PREHISTORIC FOREST

and other poems

Bryan Walters

For
Gareth
and
Arianwen
who have walked many fields with me

.... BRYAN WALTERS 1988

First published in Great Britain by
DOUGLAS McLEAN
at
THE FOREST BOOKSHOP
8 St. Johns Street, Coleford, Glos. Tel: (0594) 33858

D1328877

Prehistoric Forest or Who Will Cast the Last Stone?

Even their footprints froze
in the long winters
following the longest.

Only the cave-homes
of forgotten ancestors remained,
their floors middens
for mammoth, rhino, bison
and the scavenging hyena.

With the wildwoods
and the rising ice-cold sea
came the aspen and the willow.
With the feathery birch
came the red-deer, the wild ox,
the rooting pig

and the hunters,

all intent on survival
for a few short years -

man at the expense of the others

Only the forest remains, and twentieth-century man,
ancestors forgotten,
but still burdened

with the power to preserve
and the will to destroy.

Even God Cannot Change the Past (Agathon, 447-401 BC)

Are you interested in archaeology?
a poet friend of mine was asked.

Not at all, said he.
A boring subject.
All to do with what is past.

He extracted a cigarette;
reached for his lighter.

Found it on a rugby pitch
fifty years ago. Still works.

But it didn't.

Needs a new flint
he exclaimed.

Mesolithic man
took a sharpened stick of wood;
made fire.

He extracted the arrow-shaft
from the still-warm deer.

Needs a new flint,
he exclaimed.

Then he roasted his dinner,
content with the present,
his needs fully satisfied.

An unwitting criticism
of what is now called 'civilized'.

King Arthur's Cave (Promises)

Alright son,
so – you want your room decorated.

Yes, I'll paint a deer
with the longest antlers
on the roof of the cave,
but first you learn to make
some pointed arrow-tips
and barb-like shapes
from this stone of flint.
You'll need to hunt for food, you know.

So the six-year-old
worked daily at his task
aware of his father's visionary
inadequacies with implements
so small.

Look, father
I've made some microliths,
he said,
thus demonstrating incredible vision
of what twentieth-century archaeologists
would terminologically call
his modest efforts.
Now will you paint my wall?

Well done son,
but what about the arrow-shafts?

Got to make them straight and true.
You'll need to hunt for food, you know.
So it went on..........
Well done son,
now how about a bow?

Fortunately his father could still see
a branch of reasonable shape
and the dutiful son
deftly shaped it with
a blade of flint.

Praise was heaped upon praise
until his son learned to hunt.

Now will you paint a deer upon my wall?

Well done! Well done,
said his father (rather repetitively),
tomorrow perhaps,
(thus creating procrastination).

The story is true!

For proof,
take a look in the cave -

the painting is still not done.

Winter Field-Walking, Barnfield

Above Eastbach Court,
below the summit
of Hangerberry Hill, a field
ploughed, washed by winter's rains.

He bent down;
picked up a tiny something;
wiped it clean;
inspected it;
explained:

An arrow-tip, Mesolithic.
Probably used six thousand years
or so ago while hunting elk
or red deer, maybe boar.

Ten minutes later
he'd found several more
including the source material,
a well-worked core
of flint.

Must have been a summer camp;
too cold in winter.
He gave a sigh;
pulled his hood tight
round his ears, gave a nod
towards the north, the Wye,

and, well satisfied,
walked slowly to his 'cave'.

He switched on a luminous stalactite,
sat before the fire, poured a whisky,
took out the flints
and acted as a hunter
is expected to behave
when holding in his grasp
the piece of history
he'd just captured from the past.

Walking on a Ploughed Field Near Bream

Look, dad, a flint!

He just six years old
the arrow-head,
near six thousand -

How to comprehend
the difference in time,
the difference in age?

It *is* flint, isn't it dad?

Yes, it is, and very special too

Is it prehistoric?

Yes, *very* prehistoric.

Is it older than grandad?

Yes, much older.

More than sixty times older.

Cor........
Did they use a bow to shoot with then?

Yes.

What did they shoot with it?

Deer, maybe wild pig.

Why?

For food – because they needed food.

Dad.............?

Yes.

Why didn't they just go to the supermarket ...?

Perch Holly, Ruardean

Stonehenge
leaves me as cold
as a winter solstice.
Touched and trampled
by so many tourists,
tied with wire,
a present with no past.

No mystery here for the recipient.

It's the same with chambered,
megalithic tombs.
Scrubbed, besomed
and neatly gravelled
(key available from Tumulus Cottage)

... And Norman castles.
Who can imagine a thirteenth-century
banqueting hall or boudoir
from the shambles left
by Cromwell's powder-kegs
and cannon-balls?
The drawbridge is always open,
if it still exists,
but why are the turnstiles
always painted green?

Give me a hill
high on the forest's edge
with a ploughed field
and a view of mountains
older than prehistory.

When I picked up
the arrow-head of flint
with perfect tang and barbs
I knew that I was the first
to touch it in four thousand years.
Therein lies the magic
of communication with the past,
from the mountains to the flint-stone,
and with the one who touched it last.

Getting Away From it All, 20th century BC

They leaned against the Broad Stone,
worn, weary and knee-deep
in flint-flakes, chips and cores.
Not far away a heap
of unworked flint-stones
waiting for tomorrow's market day.

They'd come a long way,
a hundred miles and more,
and only three more days
to go – three standing stones
between the rivers
and the ways well marked.

They gathered up their merchandise,
fed hired beasts of burden
and retired to their tent;
looked out at their camp-fire;
discussed barter
and the effort spent.

Then said one with persuasion
despite a bad stammer,
determined to finish
in unheard-of English
and appalling, bad grammar:

I'm giving up trading
ahead of my time
for agriculturisation
and a life that's sublime.
Thatched house in the country,
a few sheep and oxen,
and a very clear call
to get away from it all
for a life of self-sufficiency.

They never could fathom
his lack of good rhythm,
but, just laughed and thought of:

HIPPIES.

Prehistoric Foresters

They say the Forest
belonged to the Dobunni tribe
before the Romans came -
What think you?

He paused long – his thoughts
no deeper then a scowle.

No – couldn't be.

Silures then?
You think they crossed the Wye?

He glanced west
but saw no further than the Staunton meend,
then shook his head.

Then who?

They was Foresters.
They was always Foresters.......
and Foresters be miners,
he added.

Then who occupied the great hill forts
at Welshbury, Symonds Yat and Lydney Park,
I questioned.

They was Foresters of course!

But why?

Protect the iron and the coal......
Forts be all round the Forest.
Iron be important.
People who mine it; smith it,
always be important....
and the coal.

You think that they used coal
before the Romans came?

He nodded – yes.

Even prehistoric man?
The hunters who used flint
in Mesolithic times?
But where's the evidence,
I asked.

He shuffled,
looked contemptuously away,
then used his heel to dig a hole
into the blackened earth.
He gathered brittle twigs;
struck a match,
then settled back in silence,
knowing, but unnoticing
the orange flames that changed
to green and blue.

At length,
(almost an hour had passed),
he rose and kicked
the embering twigs aside.
The stones of black beneath,
still glowed.

Scars

You came to me
with your scars,

(you had told me of them.)

Stripped of all that conceals
you lay with me

accepting my own scars,

(those seen and those undisclosed.)

We shared the compulsions
of all life,

then you left.

Left each of us quantifying

scars,

and wondering where and when

the next ones would appear.

It's the Difference

I look at you
from my difference of height;
my difference of years,

(Tyrannosaurus Rex
to a French poodle.)

I search beyond the amity
of your smile
for something amorous,

but find a quizzical look
for which I have no answer.

I'm in two minds
when one was never enough,
and two equals less than one.

I ask:
Does age and height
really make a difference?

and think of last summer
when I saw a forget-me-not
upon a tumulus

and a mole-hill
upon a mountain.

Famine

The starving
have no religion.

They look through tunnels of bone
and long, empty testaments
at the parched and un-sown earth;
the withered tree of life.

Extend their fingers
for charitable grains,
but have no hands.
Seeds fall like faith
on barren sand.

Too weak
to carry crosses,
they plant them over death.
When wood is no more
they improvise
with two bleached femurs.

A dying breed of 'actors'
for TV documentaries.
Their gods depend on gifts
from human charities.

The starving
have no religion.

Survivors learn the truth:
What doesn't enter,
when in need,
can't be expressed by mouth.

Case History

You pull me around
like baggage on wheels
through the terminals
of your life.

There is always room for me
under your seat.
When you kick me,
to make room for someone else,

I am expected to be resilient.
I revolve in "Baggage Claim"
until you remember me
and realise there is something

inside me you may need.
I am an afterthought
when in your room.
You need to be reminded

that I am left behind.
Time was I held your essentials.
Not now. Please understand
my case history. I am no longer

what I was. See that trunk
over there; leather-bound, brass lock
and security clasps. It is the new me
Push that around – if you can.

Waiting for Silence

A squirrel entered my study,
lay low,
pretended it couldn't be seen
and part-concealed itself
behind my stereo.

Terrified and mute,
it waited for a silence
to run free.

Considerately, I left,
and thought;

Why doesn't fate
do this for me?

Poem for Arianwen
(A Welsh name for a girl meaning silver-white)

My child,

if only you could remember
the first light;
the first touch.

If only you could remember
the first finger that you gripped.
The finger that traced
a life-time of love
around your womb-wet hair.

If only you could have seen
the rainbow from the moon,
silver-white and magical.
A happening so rare
that named you
as new and different -
Someone special.

If only you
had seen and felt
what I did,

you would love me
after love that made you
ended.

Suddenly With Eyes

Sometimes,
and infrequently
as a rainbow from the moon
in darkest night,
there is an unexpected happening
that transforms a moment
into a season"s celebration

Sometimes,
(and sometimes never),
you wonder whether
you will ever experience again,
and if so – when,
the unforseen and unpredicted
magic that happened once
so many years ago.

Now I know.

For what was once, now is,
like a fragrant rose that grew
through snow.

Yesterday I thought of memories.
Now I think of you.

Epithalamion

What is a circle?

A circle has no beginning;
has no end, he said.

It is endless, eternal,
therefore goes on forever,

like my love, he said,
like my love.

She replied:
So swore Romeo to Juliet

by the circled moon,
that circles round the earth, but:

Swear not by the moon
the inconstant moon,

said Juliet, that monthly changes
in her circled orb,

lest that thy love
prove likewise variable.

Then I'll love you
 as the sun, said he,

the warmest circle
that is known.

With it I will give you
 life and warm security.

Promise not so easily,
said she,

for we marry in England;
the winters are long

and the sun shines
somewhat ineffectively.

Then said he: With this ring
I thee wed, I thee wed.

Thank you, said she, that I'll accept
A circle that will never sever.

It was worn by my Nan.
In those days marriage was respected.

Something permanent.
Something that's forever.

He took the ring
and placed it on her finger.

Took the ring;

placed it on her finger.

Took the ring;

placed it on her finger.

Sounds/ (of a fire engine)

NEEEE – NAAAAA
NEEEE – NAAAAA
NEEEE – NAAAAA

Do you have to make
so much noise?

I'm a fire engine, dad.

NEEEE – NAAAAA
NEEEE – NAAAAA
NEEEE – NAAAAA

There's a fire,
it could be awful bad.

NEEEE – NAAAAA
NEE...........

Please could we have less noise,
I'm studying.

But there's a fire, dad.

Well put it out quietly, will you.
Keep your noise down.

Dad.........

What now?

Your cigarette's burning
your dressing gown.

Excuses

Can we see the dragon, dad,
the one up Probert's Lane?

It's too wet.
It's raining.
Dragons don't like rain,
it puts their fire out
(Dad's making his excuses yet again).

It's stopping, dad.
(No point explaining).
It's only spotting bits.
The wet has gone.
The dragon must be hungry, dad.
Please can we go,
we'll put our wellies on.

All right,
but twenty minutes only
and no more.
And put your wellies on outside
or there'll be mud all on the floor.
But – He won't be out today,
I tell you – It's too wet.
twenty minutes only – don't forget.

I think of sipping Carlsberg Special
at The Forge,
don duffle coat and boots,
pick up a sword,
pretend to be Saint George.

Sums

I'm
two and a half years
older than she.

I'm just six
but she's still three.
Halfs don't count
it seems,
that's why sums
are hard for me.
Three plus two plus....

Six months from now
and she'll be four.
I'll still be six.
I think sums
are silly tricks
that teacher
plays on us.